Car Trip

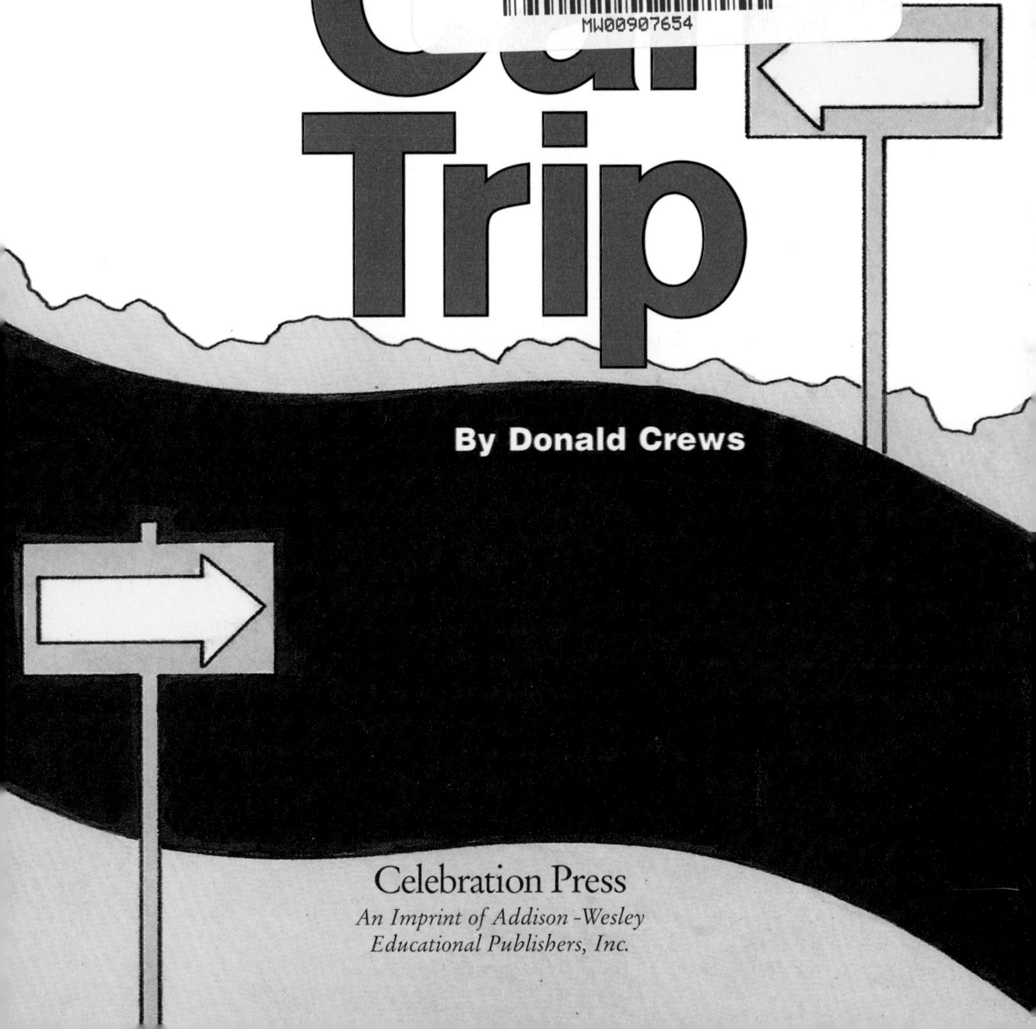

By Donald Crews

Celebration Press
An Imprint of Addison -Wesley Educational Publishers, Inc.

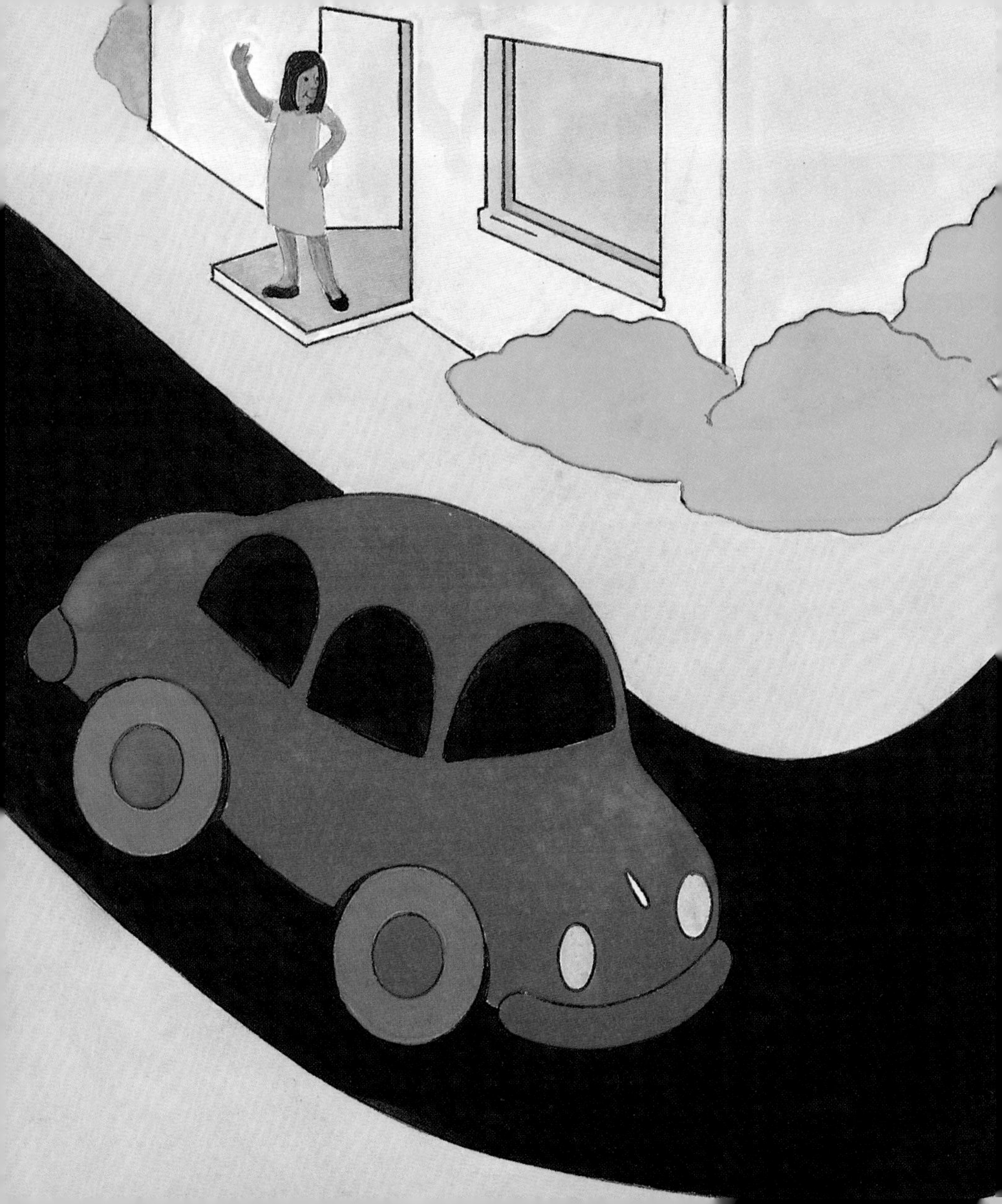

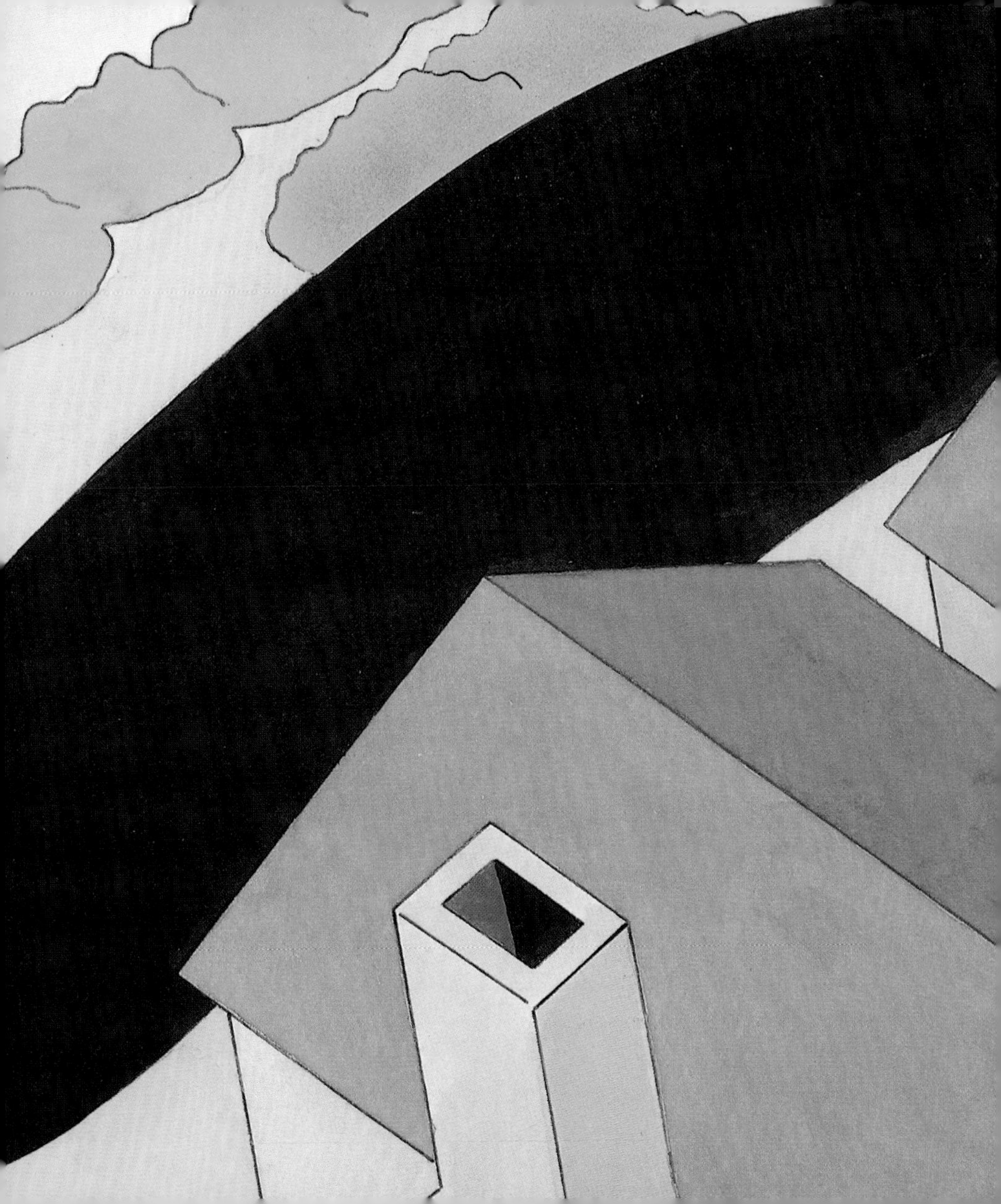

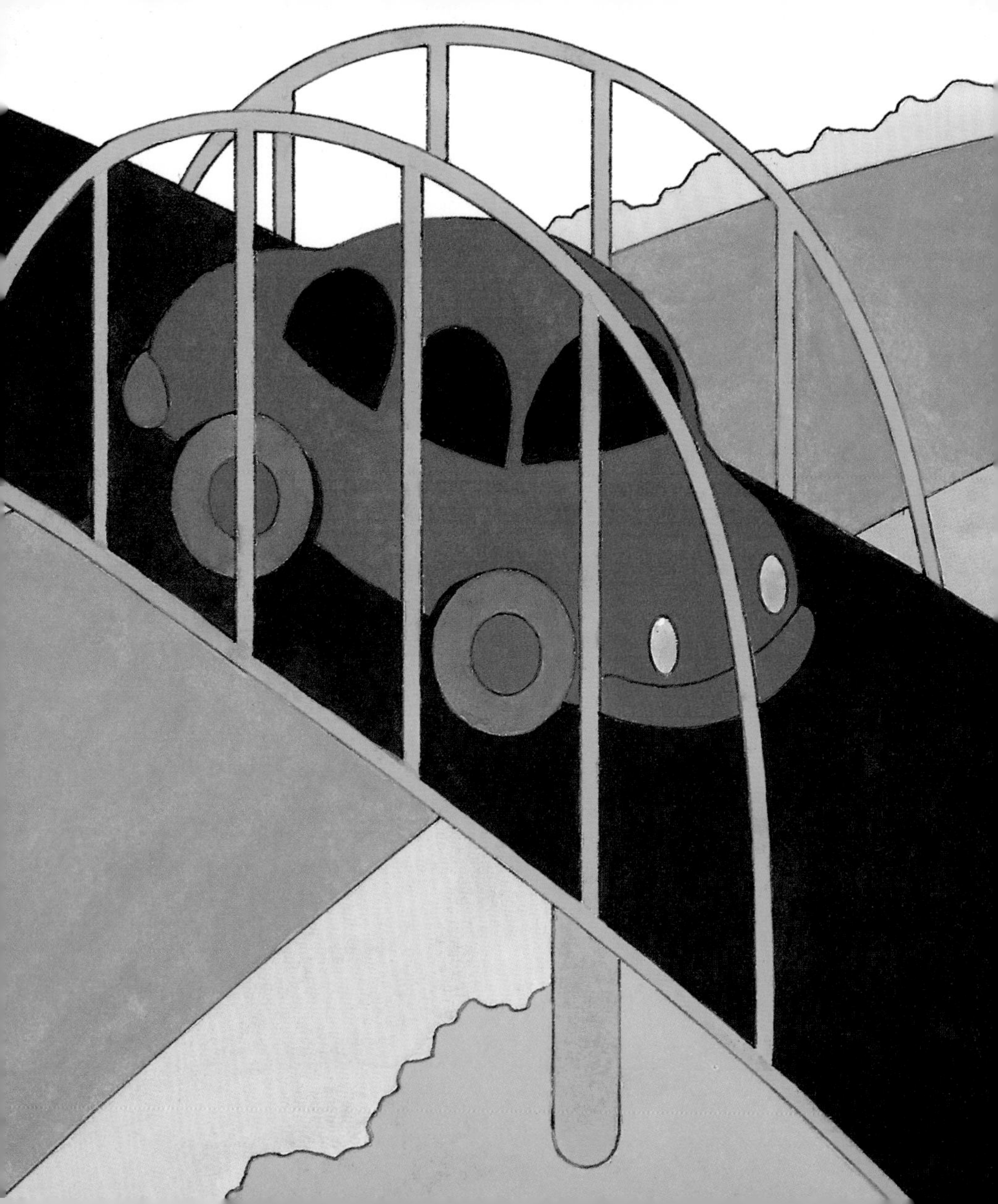

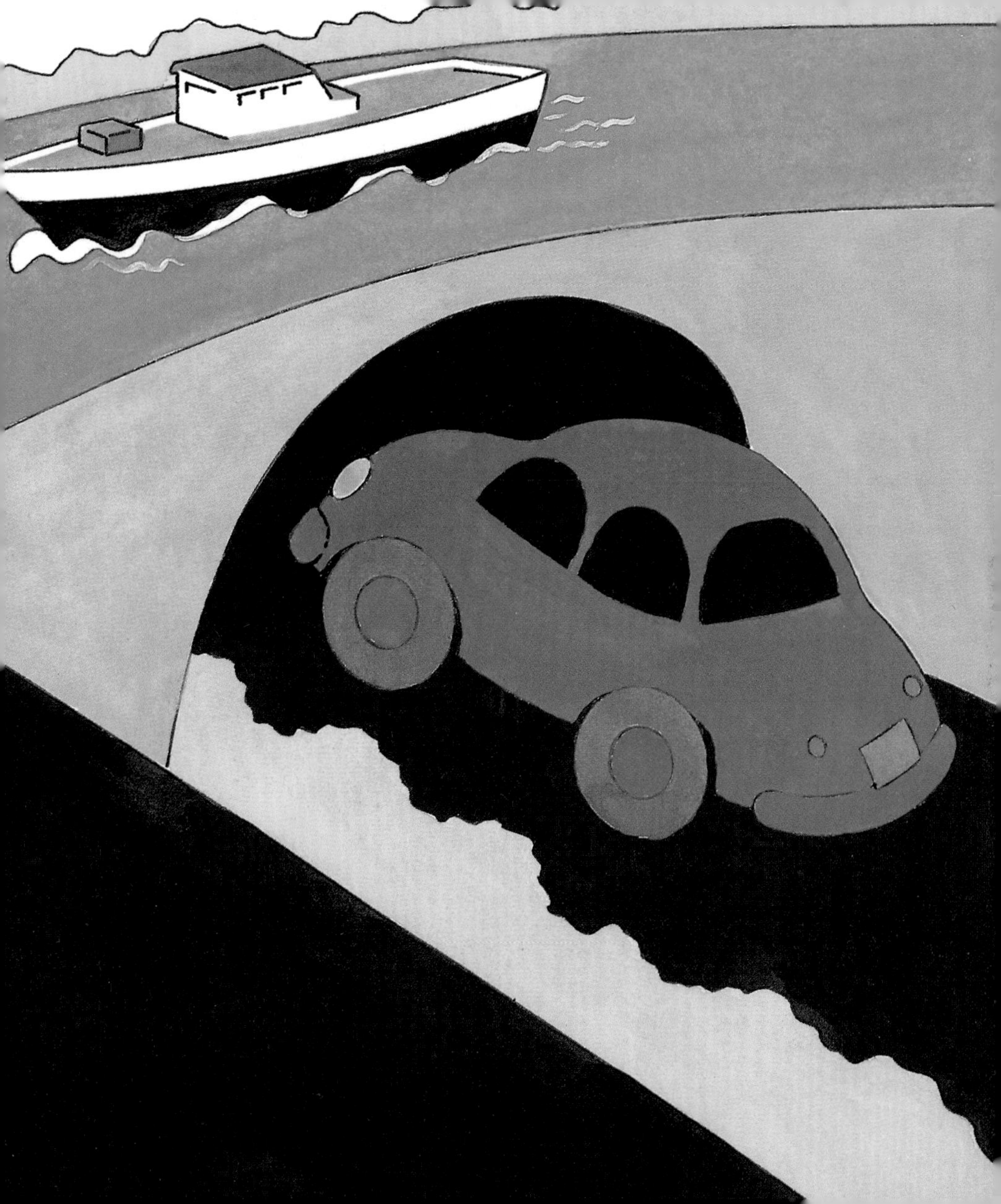

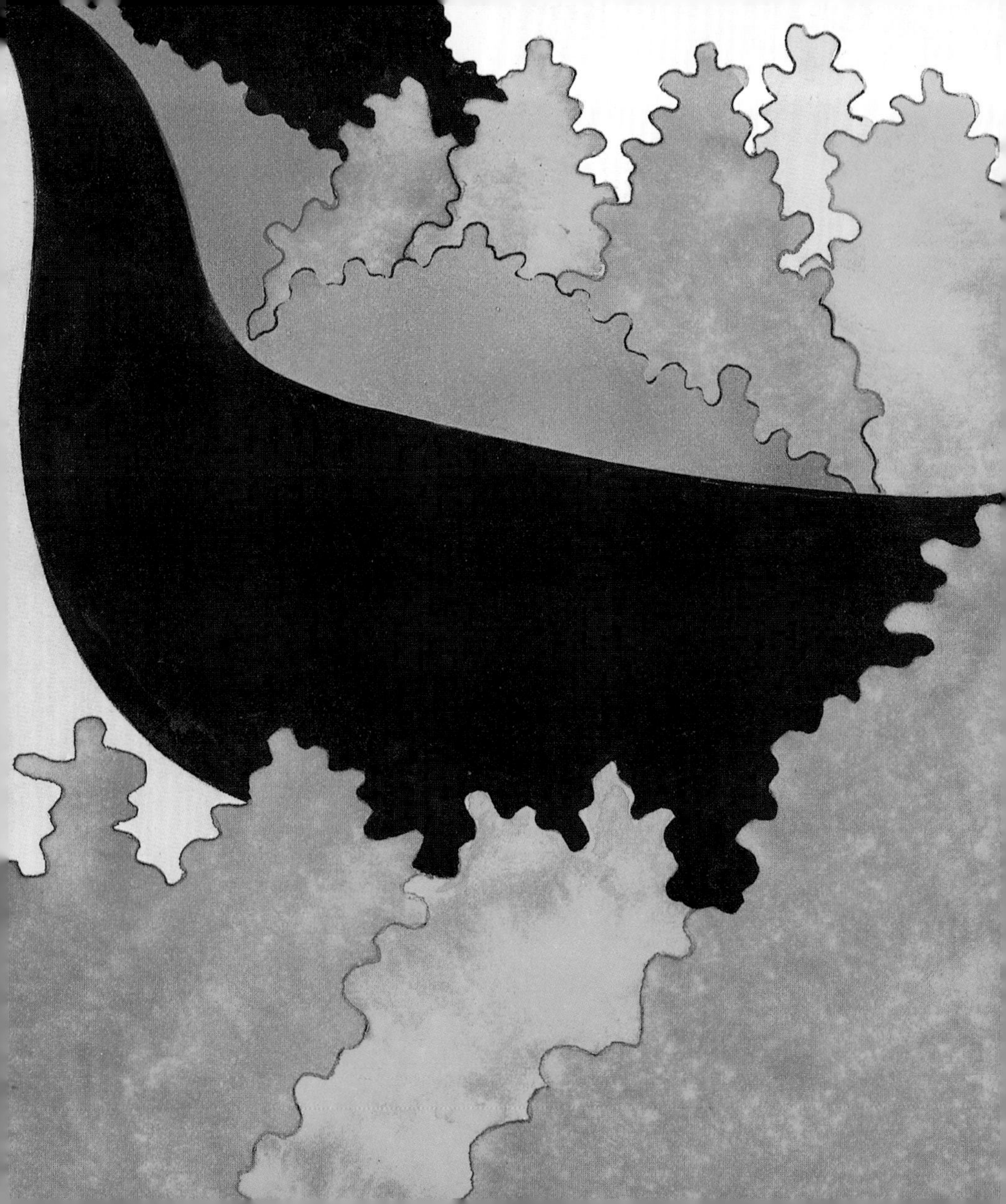

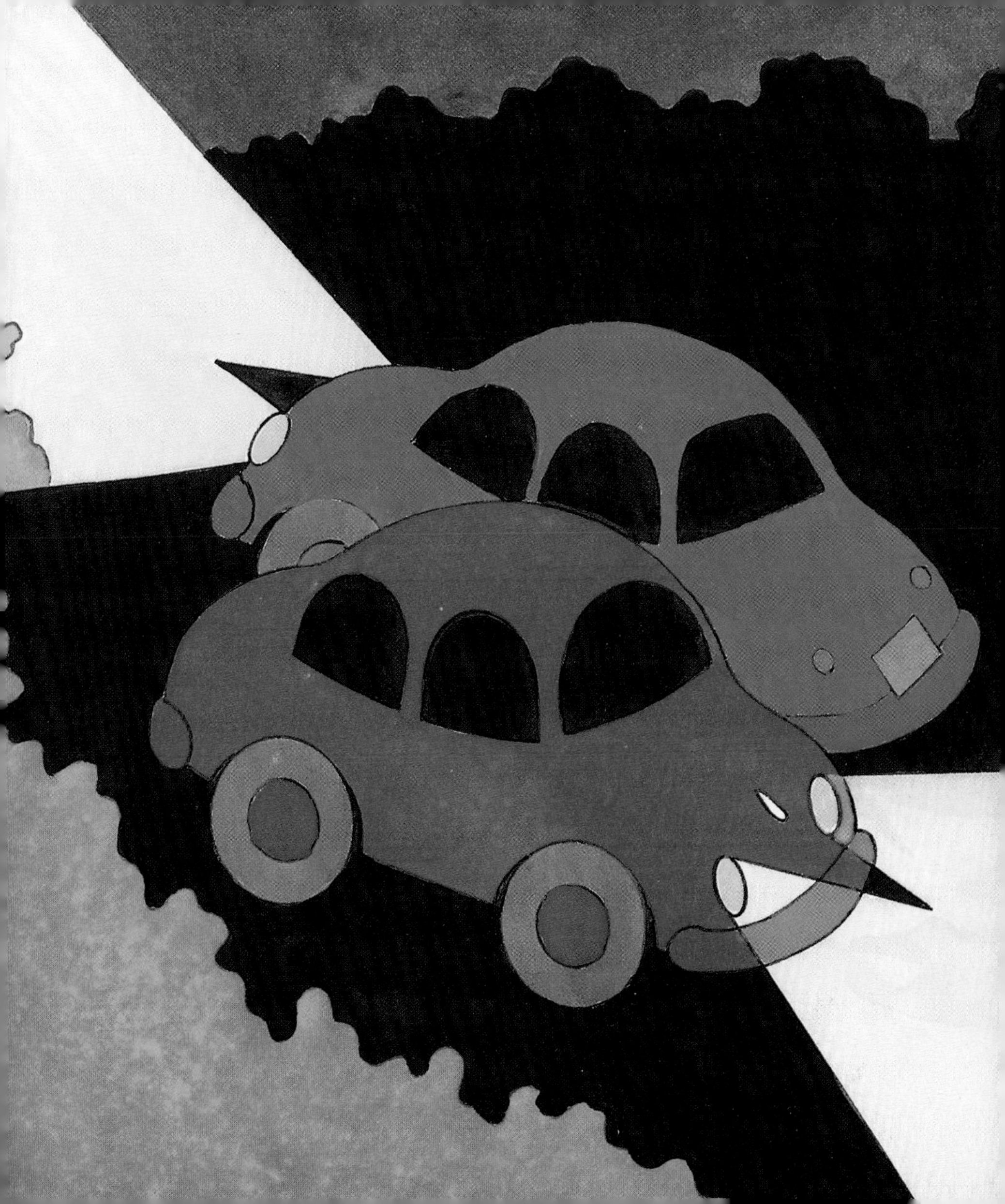

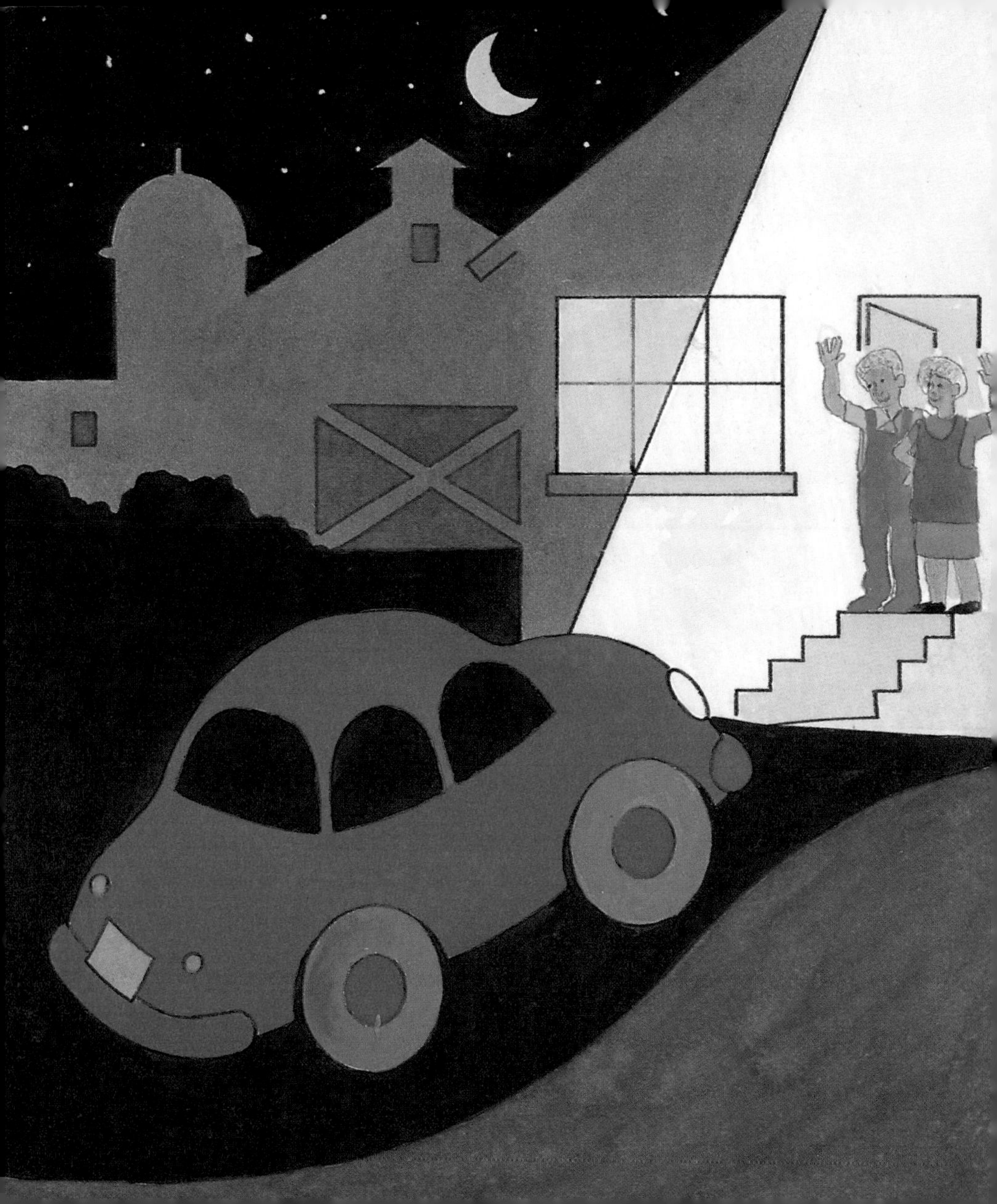